SMELL

Anita Ganeri

W
FRANKLIN WATTS
LONDON•SYDNEY

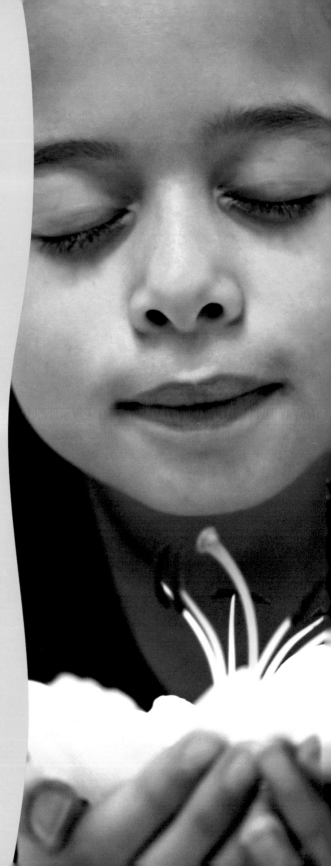

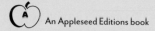 An Appleseed Editions book

First published in 2014 by Franklin Watts
338 Euston Road, London NW1 3BH

Created by Appleseed Editions Ltd,
Well House, Friars Hill, Guestling,
East Sussex TN35 4ET

Designed and illustrated by Guy Callaby
Edited by Mary-Jane Wilkins

A CIP record for this book is available from
the British Library

ISBN 978 1 4451 3156 6

Dewey Classification: 612.8'6

Picture acknowledgements
l = left, r = right, c = centre, t = top, b = bottom
page 1 Hemera/Thinkstock; 2 Juriah Mosin/Shutterstock;
3t Ann Worthy/Shutterstock, c iStockphoto/Thinkstock,
b iStockphoto/Thinkstock; 4 Jupiterimages/Getty/Thinkstock;
6 Eva Blanda/Shutterstock; 7t iStockphoto/Thinkstock,
b iStockphoto/Thinkstock; 8 Felix Mizioznikov/Shutterstock;
9 iStockphoto/Thinkstock; 10 Alenavlad/Shutterstock;
12c VStock/Thinkstock, b Jupiterimages/Getty/Thinkstock;
13 VStock/Thinkstock; 15 Jupiterimages/Getty/Thinkstock;
16 iStockphoto/Thinkstock; 17 Jupiterimages/Getty/
Thinkstock; 18 marco mayer/Shutterstock; 19 Michael Blann/
Thinkstock; 20 Juriah Mosin/Shutterstock; 21 Hemera/
Stockbyte/Thinkstock; 22t iStockphoto/Thinkstock,
b iStockphoto/Thinkstock; 23 iStockphoto/Thinkstock;
image beneath folios iStockphoto/Thinkstock
Cover: iStockphoto/Thinkstock

Printed in China

Franklin Watts is a division of Hachette Children's Books,
an Hachette UK company
www.hachette.co.uk

Contents

Super smell

What happens when you
smell a bunch of
flowers?
Do they smell
nasty or nice?

Smell is one of your senses. Your senses tell you about the world around you.

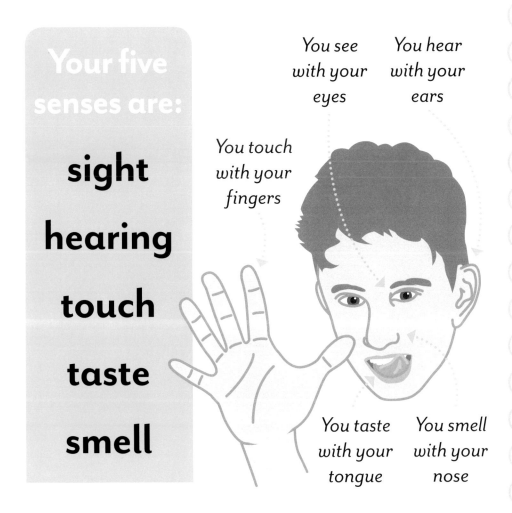

Your five senses are:

sight

hearing

touch

taste

smell

You see with your eyes

You hear with your ears

You touch with your fingers

You taste with your tongue

You smell with your nose

Favourite smells

What is your favourite smell? Do you like the smell of freshly-baked muffins?

The smell of muffins can make you feel hungry.

Do you like strong smells, like stinky cheese?

Do you like clean smells, like soap?

What are smells?

Smells are made up of tiny **bits** that float in the air. They are too small to see.

When you breathe in, these tiny bits go up your nostrils and into your nose.

The smell of these strawberries goes up your nose.

How do you smell?

The smells float up into a space inside your nose. It is called your nasal cavity.

Your nasal cavity is a space inside your head.

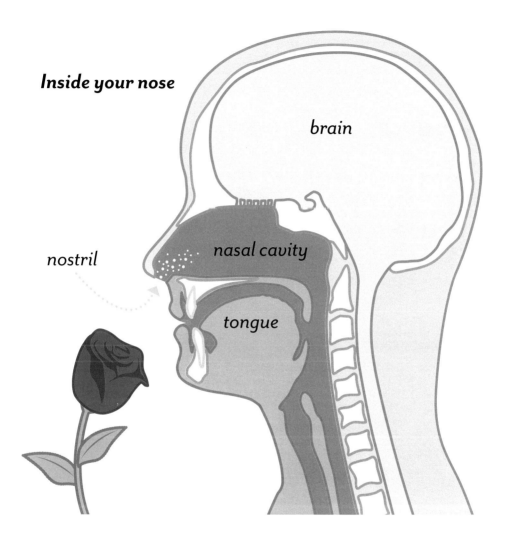

Inside your nose

brain

nostril

nasal cavity

tongue

There, special hairs catch the smells. The hairs are covered in sticky mucus.

Smelly messages

The sticky hairs send messages about the smells along nerves to your brain.

You can smell more than **3,000** different smells.

Then your brain sorts out the messages and tells you what you are smelling.

Sniff! Sniff!

Sniffing helps smells to smell stronger. When you sniff, you breathe in a big jet of air.

This jet of air carries more smells than usual to the hairs and nerves in your nose.

When you sniff, smells go straight to your nose nerves.

Wrinkly nose

Do you **wrinkle** up
your nose when you
smell something
really nasty?

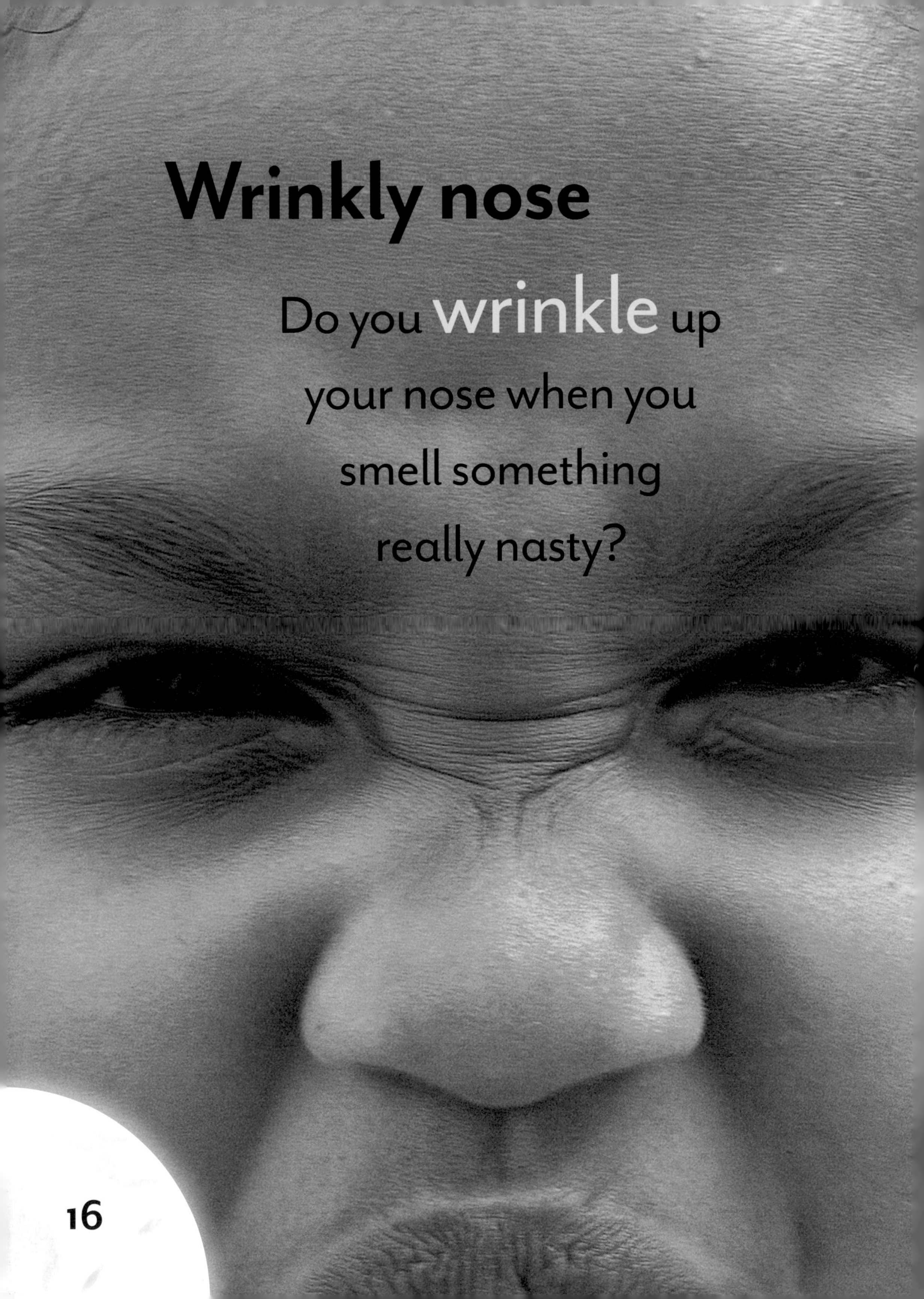

Wrinkling your nose **stops** air and smells from floating up into your nose.

Useful smells

Smells are really useful. Nice smells, like fresh pizza, can tell you that food is good to eat.

If food smells nasty, it may be bad to eat.

Some smells can warn you of **danger**. The smell of burning tells you that there is a fire.

Taste and smell

Your senses of smell and taste often work together to tell you what your food is like.

Hold your nose so that you can't smell. Then eat a piece of apple. What does it taste like?

Smell facts

A dog can smell about three million smells – that's a thousand times more than you!

Some animals use smell as weapons. A skunk sprays its enemies with a liquid that smells terrible.

Smells can remind you of things. The smell of cut grass might remind you of the summer.

Don't smell a bunch of flowers if you have **hayfever**. They will make you sneeze!

Useful words

mucus
A jelly-like slime made by the body.

nasal cavity
A space in your head behind your nose.

nerves
Thin, long wires inside your body that carry messages between your body and brain.

nostrils
The two holes at the front of your nose.

Index